DON'T
TREAD
ON
ME

DON'T
TREAD
ON
ME

AN AMERICAN PATRIOT'S BOOK OF QUOTES

Compiled and Edited by

R. BLAKE WILSON

WestView Press, LLC

Don't Tread On Me: An American Patriot's Book of Quotes
Compiled and Edited by R. Blake Wilson

© 2010 R. Blake Wilson

Although every precaution has been taken to verify the accuracy of the information contained herein, the author and publisher assume no responsibility for any errors or omissions. No liability is assumed for damages that may result from the use of information contained within.

Unless otherwise noted, images in this publication were in the public domain and obtained from the Library of Congress and Wikipedia.org

Books may be purchased in quantity and/ or special sales by contacting the publisher:
WestView Press, LLC
624 Horan Court
Castle Rock, Colorado 80108
303 718 3039
twilson523@msn.com

Cover and interior design by Nick Zelinger/NZ Graphics

Author Photo by Jimmy's Photography Castle Rock, Colorado

Library of Congress Control Number: 2010940436

ISBN: 978-0-9831406-0-3 (softcover)

First Edition

Printed in the United States of America

For more information, visit www.DontTreadOnMeBook.com

★ For The American Patriot ★

CONTENTS

Introduction

Don't Tread On Me - An American Patriot's Book of Quotes is a reminder to all patriots that the struggle in America between liberty and tyranny has been an ongoing battle. The Founders of America were triumphant in their war against the tyranny of the English King, George III. Will the patriots of today be equally triumphant? Will liberty prevail? The tyranny of today brought on by massive government growth and spending both federal, state and even county and city has exploded into a heavy burden that founder Thomas Jefferson warned against, "Democracy will cease to exist when you take away from those who are willing to work to give to those who are not."

I believe, as most others believe, that government has a vital role to play in civilized society. However, I also believe there is a Constitutional limit to the role government should participate in our lives. Ronald Reagan said it best, "Government is not the solution to our problems, government is the problem." This quote lies at the core of the fundamental battle being waged in America today. The Liberal or Progressive Democrat believes that governments role includes solving all of societies inequalities. While the Conservative Republican believes less government and private industry can best provide the foundation for our success. The Tea Party movement has established itself on the belief that both parties promote larger government and more spending. These American patriots believe, as I do, that less government is good government.

I agree with what Dennis Prager has often said on his radio program, "The bigger the government, the smaller the citizen." How can government continue to grow and grow and spend and spend and not become more a part of our lives? How can the citizen that is dependent on government for "the pursuit of happiness" not be made smaller? Remember, "A government big enough to provide you everything is big enough to take everything."

This book is a collection of quotes that I believe will inspire each reader, The American Patriot, to triumph over tyranny.

May God Bless America!

~ R. Blake Wilson

The Gadsden Flag

The Gadsden Flag is an American historical flag with a yellow field depicting a rattlesnake coiled and ready to strike. Below the snake is the legend "DONT TREAD ON ME."

The flag was designed in 1775 by the American general and statesmen Christopher Gadsden.

A Patriot's History Lesson

In the fall of 1775 the Continental Navy was established to intercept incoming British ships carrying war supplies to the British troops in the colonies. To aid in this, the Second Continental Congress authorized the mustering of five companies of Marines to accompany the Navy on their first mission. The Marines that enlisted were from Philadelphia and they carried drums painted yellow, depicting a coiled rattlesnake with thirteen rattles, and the motto "DONT TREAD ON ME." This is the first recorded mention of the future Gadsden flag's symbolism.

At the Congress, Continental Colonel Christopher Gadsden represented his home state of South Carolina. He was one of the three members of the Marine committee who were outfitting the first naval mission. It is unclear whether Gadsden took his inspiration from the Marine's drums, or if he inspired them himself.

Before the departure of that first mission, the newly appointed Commander-in-Chief of the Navy, Commodore Esek Hopkins, received the yellow rattlesnake flag from Gadsden to serve as his distinctive personal standard.

Gadsden also presented a copy of the flag to the South Carolina legislature in Charleston, South Carolina. This was recorded in the South Carolina Congressional Journals:

Colonel Gadsden presented to the Congress an elegant standard, such as is to be used by the Commander-in-Chief of the American Navy; being yellow in field, with a lively representation of a rattlesnake in the middle, in the attitude of going to strike, and these words underneath, "DONT TREAD ON ME."

The use of the timber rattlesnake as a symbol of the American Colonies can be traced back to the publications of Benjamin Franklin. In 1751, he made the first reference to the rattlesnake in a satirical commentary published in his *Pennsylvania Gazette.* It had been the policy of Britain to send convicted criminals to America, and Franklin suggested that they thank the British by sending rattlesnakes to England.

In 1775, during the French and Indian War, Franklin published his famous woodcut of a snake cut into eight sections. It represented the colonies, with New England joined together as the head and South Carolina as the tail, following their order along the coast. Under the snake was the message, "JOIN OR DIE." This was the first political cartoon published in an American newspaper.

As the American Revolution grew closer, the snake began to see more use as a symbol of the colonies. In 1774, Paul Revere added it to the title of his paper, The Massachusetts Spy, as a snake joined to fight a British dragon. In December 1775, Benjamin Franklin published an essay in the *Pennsylvania Journal* under the pseudonym American Guesser in which he suggested that the rattlesnake was a good symbol for the American spirit:

> *I recollected that her eye excelled in brightness, that of any other animal, and that she has no eye lids. - She may therefore be esteemed an emblem of vigilance. - She never begins an attack, nor, when once engaged, ever surrenders: She is therefore an emblem of magnanimity and true courage. - As*

if anxious to prevent all pretensions of quarreling with her, the weapons with which nature has furnished her, she conceals in the roof of her mouth, so that , to those who are unacquainted with her, she appears to be a most defenseless animal: and even when those weapons are shown and extended for her defense, they appear weak and contemptible: but the wounds however small, are decisive and fatal: - Conscious of this, she never wounds till she has generously given notice, even to her enemy, and cautioned him against the danger of treading on her. - Was I wrong, Sir, in thinking this a strong picture of the temper and conduct of America?"

Today the Gadsden Flag is considered one of the first flags of the United States. Since the American Revolution the flag has been used as a symbol of American Patriotism.

Abraham Lincoln
1809-1865
16th American President

NO. 1

Be sure you put your feet in the right place, then stand firm.

~ Abraham Lincoln

NO. 2

Any people anywhere,
being inclined and having the power,
have the right to rise up, and shake off
the existing government, and form a new
one that suits them better. This is a most
valuable - a most sacred right - a right, which
we hope and believe, is to liberate the world.

~ Abraham Lincoln

NO. 3

America will never
be destroyed from the
outside. If we falter
and lose our freedoms,
it will be because
we destroyed ourselves.

~ Abraham Lincoln

NO. 4

My concern is not whether
God is on our side;
my concern is to be
on God's side.

~ Abraham Lincoln

NO. 5

Those who deny
freedom to others
deserve it not
for themselves.

~ Abraham Lincoln

NO. 6

I like to see a man proud
of the place in which he lives.
I like to see a man live
so that his place will be
proud of him.

~ Abraham Lincoln

NO. 7

WE THE PEOPLE

are the rightful masters of
both Congress and the Courts,
not to overthrow the Constitution
but to overthrow the men
who would pervert
the Constitution.

~ Abraham Lincoln

NO. 8

We cannot help the poor
by tearing down the rich.
You cannot help the
wage earner by hurting
the wage payer.

~ Abraham Lincoln

NO. 9

At what point is the approach of danger
to be expected? I answer, if it ever
reach us, it must spring up amongst us.
If destruction be our lot, we must
ourselves be its author and finisher.
As a nation of free men, we must live
through all time or die by suicide.

~ Abraham Lincoln

NO. 10

WE ALL DECLARE FOR LIBERTY;

but in using the same word we do not all mean
the same thing. With some the word *liberty* may
mean for each man to do as he pleases with himself,
and the product of his labor; while others,
the same word may mean for some men to do
as they please with other men, and the product
of other men's labor. Here are two, not only
different, but incompatible things, called the
same name – *liberty*. And it follows that each
of these things is, by the respective parties,
called by two different and incompatible
names – *liberty and tyranny.*

~ Abraham Lincoln

Adlai Stevenson
1900-1965
American Politician

NO. 11

A free society is one where it is safe to be unpopular.

~ Adlai Stevenson

Albert Camus
1913-1960
French Algerian Author

NO. 12

Freedom is nothing else but a chance to be better.

~ Albert Camus

Albert Einstein
1879-1955
Physicist and Philosopher

NO. 13

Everything that is really great and inspiring is created by the individual who can labor in freedom.

~ Albert Einstein

NO. 14

The hardest thing in the world to understand is the income tax.

~ Albert Einstein

Alexis de Tocqueville
1805-1859
French Political Scientist

NO. 15

Democracy and socialism have nothing
in common but one word: *equality*.
But notice the difference: while democracy
seeks equality in *liberty*, socialism seeks
equality in *servitude*.

~ Alexis de Tocqueville

Archibald MacLeish
1892-1982
American Poet & Writer

NO. 16

There are those, I know, who will say
that the liberation of humanity,
the freedom of man and mind,
is nothing but a dream.
They are right. It is the American Dream.

~ Archibald MacLeish

Aristotle
384 B.C. - 322 B.C.
Greek Philosopher

NO. 17

The basis of a democratic state is liberty.

~ Aristotle

Benjamin Franklin
1706-1790
American Founding Father

NO. 18

Only a virtuous people are capable
of freedom. As nations become corrupt
and vicious, they have more need of masters.

~ Benjamin Franklin

NO. 19

Whoever would overthrow the liberty
of a nation must begin by subduing
the freeness of speech.

~ Benjamin Franklin

NO. 20

Any society that would give up
a little liberty to gain a little security will
deserve neither and lose both.

~ Benjamin Franklin

NO. 21

A great empire, like a great cake,
is most easily diminished at the edges.

~ Benjamin Franklin

NO. 22

God grant that not only the love of liberty
but a thorough knowledge of the rights
of man may pervade all nations of the earth,
so that a philosopher may set his foot anywhere
on its surface and say: "This is my country."

~ Benjamin Franklin

NO. 23

Where liberty dwells, there is my country.

~ Benjamin Franklin

NO. 24

They that give up essential liberty
to obtain a little temporary safety
deserve neither liberty or safety.

~ Benjamin Franklin

NO. 25

Never spend your money
before you have earned it.

~ Benjamin Franklin

NO. 26

The Constitution only gives people
the right to pursue happiness.
You have to catch it yourself.

~ Benjamin Franklin

Benjamin Rush
1745-1813
American Founding Father

NO. 27

By removing the Bible from the schools
we would be wasting so much time and money
in punishing criminals and so little pains to
prevent crime. Take the Bible out of our schools
and there would be an explosion in crime.

~ Benjamin Rush

Carl Schurz
1829-1906
American Statesman & Union Army General

NO. 28

My Country, right or wrong;
if right, to be kept right;
and if wrong, to be set right.

~ Carl Schurz

Calvin Coolidge
1872-1933
30th American President

NO. 29

Collecting more taxes than is absolutely
necessary is legalized robbery.

~ Calvin Coolidge

NO. 30

Patriotism is easy
to understand in America -
it means looking out for yourself
by looking out for your country.

~ Calvin Coolidge

Charles Kingsley
1819-1875
English Clergyman, Professor & Historian

NO. 31

There are two freedoms - the false,
where a man is free to do what he likes;
the true, where he is free to do what he ought.

~ Charles Kingsley

Daniel Webster
1782-1852
American Statesman

NO. 32

Liberty and Union, now and forever, one and inseparable!

~ Daniel Webster

NO. 33

There is no nation on earth
powerful enough to accomplish our overthrow.
Our destruction, should it come at all, will be
from another quarter. From the inattention of
the people to the concerns of their government,
from their carelessness and negligence.
I fear that they may place too implicit a
confidence in their public servants and
fail properly to scrutinize their conduct that
in this way they may become the instruments
of their own undoing.

~ Daniel Webster

David Hume
1711-1776
Scottish Philosopher and Historian

NO. 34

It is seldom that liberty of any kind
is lost all at once.

~ David Hume

Declaration of Independence
July 4th, 1776

NO. 35

Governments are instituted among men,
deriving their powers from
the consent of the governed.

~ Declaration of Independence

Dennis Prager
Talk Radio Host

NO. 36

The bigger the government....
the smaller the citizen.

~ Dennis Prager

Dwight D. Eisenhower
1890-1969
34th President of the United States

NO. 37

History does not long entrust the
care of freedom to the weak or the timid.

~ Dwight D. Eisenhower

NO. 38

Here in America

we descended in blood and in spirit from
revolutionists and rebels - men and women who
dare to dissent from accepted doctrine.
As their heirs, may we never confuse
honest dissent with disloyal subversion.

~ Dwight D. Eisenhower

Edmund Burke
1729-1797
Irish Statesman & Author

NO. 39

The people never give up their liberties
but under some delusion.

~ Edmund Burke

Elias Boudinot
1740-1821
American Statesman

NO. 40

Good government generally begins in the family, and if the moral character of a people once degenerate, their political character must soon follow.

~ Elias Boudinot

Elmer Davis
1890-1958
Author & News Reporter

NO. 41

This nation will remain the land of the free only as long as it is the home of the brave.

~ Elmer Davis

Felix Frankfurter
1882 -1965
Associate Justice of the United States Supreme Court

NO. 42

We have enjoyed so much freedom
for so long that we are perhaps in danger
of forgetting how much blood it cost
to establish the Bill of Rights.

~ Felix Frankfurter

Franklin D. Roosevelt
1882-1945
32nd American President

NO. 43

In the truest sense, freedom cannot be bestowed; it must be achieved.

~ Franklin D. Roosevelt

NO. 44

True individual freedom cannot exist
without economic security and independence.
People who are hungry and out of a job are
the stuff of which dictatorships are made.

~ Franklin D. Roosevelt

Friedrich Nietzsche
1844-1900
German Philosopher

NO. 45

Freedom is the will to be responsible to ourselves.

~ Friedrich Nietzsche

Gary Hart
Politician

NO. 46

I think there is one higher office than President and I would call it Patriot.

~ Gary Hart

George Savile
1633-1695
English Statesman

NO. 47

When the People contend for their liberty,
they seldom get anything for their victory
but new masters.

~ George Savile

George Bernard Shaw
1856-1950
Irish Playwright
Co-founder London School of Economics

NO. 48

Liberty means responsibility. That is why most men dread it.

~ George Bernard Shaw

George Washington
1732-1799
1st American President

NO. 49

The time is near at hand which must determine whether Americans are to be free men or slaves.

~ George Washington

NO. 50

The marvel of all history
is the patience with which men and women
submit to burdens unnecessarily laid
upon them by their governments.

~ George Washington

NO. 51

The preservation of the sacred fire of liberty
and the destiny of the republican model
of government are justly considered....
staked on the experiment entrusted to
the hands of the American people.

~ George Washington

NO. 52

Liberty,
when it takes root,
is a plant of rapid growth.

~ George Washington

NO. 53

If we desire to avoid insult, we must be able to
repel it; if we desire to secure peace, one of
the most powerful instruments of our rising
prosperity, it must be known, that we are
at all times ready for War.

~ George Washington

NO. 54

Firearms are second only
to the Constitution in importance;
they are the peoples' liberty's teeth.

~ George Washington

NO. 55

Government is not reason,
it is not eloquent; it is force.
Like fire, it is a dangerous servant
and a fearful master.

~ George Washington

NO. 56

If the freedom of speech is taken away
then dumb and silent we may be led,
like sheep to slaughter.

~ George Washington

NO. 57

It is impossible to rightly govern
a nation without God and the Bible.

~ George Washington

NO. 58

Arbitrary power is most easily
established on the ruins of
Liberty abused to Licentiousness.

~ George Washington

Hubert H. Humphrey
1911-1978
38th Vice President of the United States

NO. 59

What we need are critical lovers of
America - patriots who express their faith
in their country by working to improve it."

~ Hubert H. Humphrey

James Madison
1751-1836
4th American President

NO. 60

I believe there are more instances of the abridgment of the freedom of the people by gradual and silent encroachments of those in power than by violent and sudden usurpations.

~ James Madison

NO. 61

The essence of government is power;
and power, lodged as it must in human hands,
will ever be liable to abuse.

~ James Madison

NO. 62

In republics, the great danger is,
that the majority may not sufficiently
respect the rights of the minority.

~ James Madison

NO. 63

The advancement and diffusion
of knowledge is the only guardian
of true liberty.

~ James Madison

NO. 64

Americans have the right and advantage
of being armed - unlike the citizens of
other countries whose governments
are afraid to trust the people with arms.

~ James Madison

Jean-Baptist Colbert
1619-1683
French Minister of Finance

NO. 65

The art of taxation

consists in so plucking the goose
as to obtain the largest amount of feathers
with the least amount of hissing.

~ Jean-Baptist Colbert

John Adams
1735-1826
2nd American President

NO. 66

There is danger from all men.
The only maxim of a free government
ought to be to trust no man living with
the power to endanger the public liberty.

~ John Adams

NO. 67

Remember, democracy never lasts long.
It soon wastes, exhausts, and murders itself.
There was never a democracy that
did not commit suicide.

~ John Adams

NO. 68

Liberty cannot be preserved without a general
knowledge among the people, who have a right,
and indisputable, unalienable, indefeasible,
divine right to that most dreaded and envied
kind of knowledge, I mean, the character
and conduct of their rulers.

~ John Adams

NO. 69

Children should be educated and instructed
in the principles of freedom.

~ John Adams

John S. Calhoun
1782-1850
7th Vice-President of United States

NO. 70

Irresponsible power is inconsistent
with liberty, and must corrupt those
who exercise it.

~ John S. Calhoun

John S. Coleman
American Politician

NO. 71

The point to remember is that what government gives...it must first take away.

~ John S. Coleman

John Philpot Curran
1750-1817
Irish Orator & Politician

NO. 72

The condition upon which God hath given
liberty to man is eternal vigilance.

~ John Philpot Curran

John Gunther
1901-1970
American Journalist

NO. 73

Ours is the only country deliberately
founded on a good idea.

~ John Gunther

John F. Kennedy
1917-1963
35th American President

NO. 74

My fellow Americans,

ask not what your country can do for you,
ask what you can do for your country.

~ John F. Kennedy

NO. 75

The tax on capital gains directly affects
investment decisions, the mobility and flow of risk
capital, the ease or difficulty experienced
by new ventures in obtaining capital,
and thereby the strength and potential
for growth in the economy.

~ John F. Kennedy

John Milton
1608-1674
English Poet & Author

NO. 76

Nations grown corrupt;

Love bondage more than liberty;

bondage with ease than strenuous liberty.

~ John Milton

NO. 77

Give me the liberty to know,
to utter, and to argue freely according
to conscience, above all liberties.

~ John Milton

John Wayne
1907-1979
American Film Actor

NO. 78

Sure, I wave the American flag.
Do you know a better flag to wave?
Sure, I love my country with all her faults.
I am not ashamed of that, never have been,
never will be.

~ John Wayne

John Winthrop
1588-1649
Governor of the Massachusetts Bay Colony

NO. 79

Liberty is the proper end and object of authority, and cannot subsist without it; and it is liberty to that which is good, just, and honest.

~ John Winthrop

Lee Greenwood
Country Music Artist

NO. 80

And I'm proud to be an American,
where at least I know I'm free.
And I won't forget the men who died,
who gave that right to me.

~ Lee Greenwood

Leon Panetta
CIA Director

NO. 81

If we don't do something to simplify
the tax system, we're going to end up
with a national police force
of internal revenue agents.

~ Leon Panetta

David Lloyd George
1863-1945
British Prime Minister

NO. 82

Liberty has restraints but no frontiers.

~ David Lloyd George

Lord Acton
1834-1902
English Historian

NO. 83

Liberty is not a means to a higher political end.
It is itself the highest political end.

~ Lord Acton

Louis D. Brandeis
1856-1941
Associate Justice of the United States Supreme Court

NO. 84

The greatest dangers to liberty
lurk in insidious encroachments by men of zeal,
well-meaning but without understanding.

~ Louis D. Brandeis

NO. 85

Those who won our independence believed liberty
to be the secret of happiness and courage
to be the secret of liberty.

~ Louis D. Brandeis

Mark Twain
1835-1910
American Author & Humorist

NO. 86

Each man must himself alone decide what is right
and what is wrong, which course is patriotic and
which isn't. You cannot shirk this and be a man.
To decide against your conviction is to be an
unqualified and excusable traitor, both to yourself
and to your country, let men label you as they may.

~ Mark Twain

NO. 87

The only difference between a tax man
and a taxidermist is that the
taxidermist leaves the skin.

~ Mark Twain

NO. 88

Patriotism is supporting your country
all of the time, and your government
when it deserves it.

~ Mark Twain

Margaret Thatcher
British Prime Minister

NO. 89

Europe was created by history.
America was created by philosophy.

~ Margaret Thatcher

Martin Luther King Jr.
1929-1968
American Civil Rights Leader

NO. 90

Freedom is never voluntarily given by the oppressor; it must be demanded by the oppressed.

~ Martin Luther King Jr.

Marilyn vos Savant
American Magazine Columnist

NO. 91

What is the essence of America?
Finding and maintaining that perfect,
delicate balance between freedom "to"
and freedom "from."

~ Marilyn vos Savant

Milton Friedman
1912-2006
American Economist

NO. 92

Government can raise taxes because
it can persuade a sizable fraction of
the populace that somebody else will pay.

~ Milton Friedman

Napoleon Bonaparte
1769-1821
Emperor of the French

NO. 93

Among those who dislike oppression
are many who like to oppress.

~ Napoleon Bonaparte

Nathan Hale
1755-1776
American Hero

NO. 94

I only regret that I have but one life
to lose for my country.

~ Nathan Hale

Nelson Mandela
President of South Africa

NO. 95

For to be free is not merely to cast off
one's chains, but to live in a way that respects
and enhances the freedom of others.

~ Nelson Mandela

Newt Gingrich
American Politician, College Professor,
Historian & Author

NO. 96

I believe we are now in a struggle over whether
or not we are going to save America.

~ Newt Gingrich

Noah Webster
1758-1843
Father of American Scholarship & Education

NO. 97

Corrupt or incompetent men will be appointed
to execute the laws; the public revenues will be
squandered on unworthy men; and the rights
of the citizens will be violated and disregarded.

~ Noah Webster

Patrick Henry
1736-1799
1st and 6th Governor of Virginia

NO. 98

The liberties of a people never were,
nor ever will be, secure, when the transactions
of their rulers may be concealed from them.

~ Patrick Henry

NO. 99

Guard with jealous attention the public liberty.
Suspect everyone who approaches that jewel.
Unfortunately, nothing will preserve it but
downright force. Whenever you give up
that force you are ruined.

~ Patrick Henry

NO. 100

Gentlemen may cry, Peace, Peace...but there is no peace.
The war is actually begun! The next gale that sweeps
from the north will bring to our ears the clash of
resounding arms! Our brethren are already in
the field! Why stand we here idle? What is it that
gentlemen wish? What would they have?
Is life so dear, or peace so sweet, as to be
purchased at the price of chains and slavery??
Forbid it, Almighty God! I know not what course
others may take: but as for me,

"Give me Liberty or give me Death!"

~ Patrick Henry

NO. 101

Perfect freedom is as necessary to the health and vigor of commerce as it is to the health and vigor of citizenship.

~ Patrick Henry

Ralph Waldo Emerson
1803-1882
American Philosopher, Lecturer,
Essayist & Poet

NO. 102

America is another name for opportunity.
Our whole history appears like a last effort of
divine providence on behalf of the human race.

~ Ralph Waldo Emerson

Richard M. Nixon
1913-1994
37th President of the United States

NO. 103

We must always remember that America is a
great nation today not because of what government
did for people but because of what people did
for themselves and for one another.

~ Richard M. Nixon

Robert Frost
1874-1963
American Poet

NO. 104

You have freedom
when you're easy in your harness.

~ Robert Frost

Robert A. Heinlein
1907-1988
American Science Fiction Author

NO. 105

There is no worse tyranny than to force a man
to pay for what he does not want merely
because you think it would be good for him.

~ Robert A. Heinlein

Robert Ingersoll
1833-1899
Civil War Veteran & Political Leader

NO. 106

He loves his country best
who strives to make it best.

~ Robert Ingersoll

Robert J. McCracken
Clergyman

NO. 107

We on this continent should never forget
that men first crossed the Atlantic
not to find soil for their ploughs
but to secure liberty for their souls.

~ Robert J. McCracken

Ron Paul
Physician and U.S. Congressman

NO. 108

Deficits mean future tax increases,
pure and simple. Deficit spending should
be viewed as a tax on future generations.

~ Ron Paul

NO. 109

Capitalism should not be condemned,
since we haven't had capitalism.

~ Ron Paul

Ronald Reagan
1911-2004
40th American President

NO. 110

Concentrated power has always been
the enemy of liberty.

~ Ronald Reagan

NO. 111

The most terrifying words
in the English language are:
I'm from the government
and I'm here to help.

~ Ronald Reagan

NO. 112

Government's view of the economy
could be summed up in a few short phrases:
If it moves...tax it.
If it keeps moving ...regulate it.
And if it stops moving...subsidize it.

~ Ronald Reagan

NO. 113

The problem is not that people
are taxed too little, the problem
is that government spends too much.

~ Ronald Reagan

NO. 114

Freedom is never more than one generation away
from extinction. We didn't pass it to our children
in the bloodstream. It must be fought for,
protected, and handed on for them to do the same.

~ Ronald Reagan

NO. 115

The taxpayer:

That's someone who works for the
federal government, but doesn't have
to take a civil service examination.

~ Ronald Reagan

NO. 116

No government ever voluntarily reduces itself
in size. Government programs, once launched,
never disappear. Actually, a government bureau
is the nearest thing to eternal life
we'll ever see on this earth!

~ Ronald Reagan

NO. 117

Man is not free unless government is limited.

~ Ronald Reagan

Rush Limbaugh
Conservative Talk Radio Host

NO. 118

If Thomas Jefferson thought
taxation without representation was bad,
he should see how it is with representation.

~ Rush Limbaugh

Samuel Adams
1722-1803
American Patriot and Politician

NO. 119

If ye love wealth greater than liberty,
the tranquility of servitude greater than
the animating contest for freedom,
go home from us in peace.
We seek not your counsel, nor your arms.
Crouch down and lick the hand that feeds you;
May your chains set lightly upon you,
and may posterity forget that ye were our countrymen.

~ Samuel Adams

NO. 120

It is the interest of tyrants to reduce the people to ignorance and vice. For they cannot live in any country where virtue and knowledge prevail.

~ Samuel Adams

NO. 121

We have proclaimed to the world our determination to die free men, rather than to live slaves.

~ Samuel Adams

Socrates
469 B.C. - 399 B.C.
Greek Philosopher

NO. 122

People demand freedom of speech
to make up for the freedom of thought which they avoid.

~ Socrates

Theodore Roosevelt
1858-1919
26th American President

NO. 123

Every immigrant who comes to America should be required within five years to learn English or leave the country.

~ Theodore Roosevelt

Thomas Jefferson
1743-1826
3rd American President

NO. 124

I would rather be exposed to the inconveniences
of too much liberty than to those attending
too small a degree of it.

~ Thomas Jefferson

NO. 125

No free man shall ever be debarred the use of arms.

~ Thomas Jefferson

NO. 126

The two enemies of the people are criminals and government,

so let us tie the second down with the chains of the Constitution so the second will not become the legalized version of the first.

~ Thomas Jefferson

NO. 127

My God! How little do my countrymen know
what precious blessings they are in possession of,
and which no other people on earth enjoy!

~ Thomas Jefferson

NO. 128

Evil triumphs when good men do nothing.

~ Thomas Jefferson

NO. 129

When all government, domestic and foreign,
in little as in great things, shall be drawn to
Washington as the center of all power,
it will....become as venal and oppressive
as the government from which we separated.

~ Thomas Jefferson

NO. 130

The Constitution is a mere thing of wax
in the hands of the judiciary, which they may
twist and shape into any form they please.

~ Thomas Jefferson

NO. 131

The spirit of resistance
to government is so valuable on certain occasions,
that I wish it to be always kept alive.
It will often be exercised when wrong
but better so than not to be exercised at all.
I like a little rebellion now and then.
It is like a storm in the atmosphere.

~ Thomas Jefferson

NO. 132

It is error alone which needs the support
of government. Truth can stand on its own.

~ Thomas Jefferson

NO. 133

Yes, we did produce a near-perfect republic.
But will they keep it? Or will they, in the
enjoyment of plenty, lose the memory of freedom?
Material abundance without character
is the path to destruction.

~ Thomas Jefferson

NO. 134

We hold these truths to be sacred and undeniable, that all men are created equal and independent, that from that creation they derive rights inherent and inalienable, among which are the preservation of life, and liberty, and the pursuit of happiness.

~ Thomas Jefferson

NO. 135

My reading of history convinces me
that most bad governments result
from too much government.

~ Thomas Jefferson

NO. 136

I predict future happiness for Americans
if they can prevent the government from wasting
the labors of the people under the pretense
of taking care of them.

~ Thomas Jefferson

NO. 137

I am for a government rigorously frugal and simple,
applying all the possible savings of the public
revenue to the discharge of the national debt.

~ Thomas Jefferson

NO. 138

A wise and frugal government,
which shall leave men free to regulate their
own pursuits of industry and improvements,
and shall not take from the mouth of labor
the bread it has earned, this is the sum of
good government.

~ Thomas Jefferson

NO. 139

All tyranny needs to gain a foothold
is for the people of good conscience
to remain silent.

~ Thomas Jefferson

NO. 140

When governments fear the people
there is liberty.
When the people fear the government
there is tyranny.

~ Thomas Jefferson

NO. 141

Experience has shown, that even under
the best forms of government those entrusted
with power, in time, and by slow operations,
perverted it into tyranny.

~ Thomas Jefferson

NO. 142

If the present Congress errors in too much talking,
how can it be otherwise in a body to which
the people send one hundred and fifty lawyers,
whose trade it is to question everything,
yield nothing, and talk by the hour.

~ Thomas Jefferson

NO. 143

No government ought to be without censors;
and where the press is free no one ever will.

~ Thomas Jefferson

NO. 144

Single acts of tyranny may be ascribed to the accidental opinion of the day; but a series of oppressions, begun at a distinguished period, and pursued unalterably through every change of administration too plainly proves a deliberate, systematic plan of reducing us to slavery.

~ Thomas Jefferson

NO. 145

The tree of liberty must be refreshed
from time to time with the blood
of patriots and tyrants.

~ Thomas Jefferson

NO. 146

Democracy will cease to exist

when you take away from those who are willing
to work to give to those who are not.

~ Thomas Jefferson

NO. 147

We must not let our rulers load us with perpetual debt. We must make our election between economy and liberty or profusion and servitude. If we run into such debt, as that we must be taxed in our meat and in our drink, in our necessaries and our comforts, in our labors and our amusements, for our calling and our creeds.

We will have no time to think, no means of calling our miss managers to account but be glad to obtain subsistence by hiring ourselves to rivet their chains on the necks of our fellow sufferers. And this is the tendency of all human governments.

A departure from principle in one instance becomes a precedent for another..till the bulk of society is reduced to be mere automations of misery. And the fore-horse of this frightful team is public debt.

Taxation follows that, and in its train wretchedness and oppression.

~ Thomas Jefferson

Thomas Paine
1737-1809
Founding Father of America

NO. 148

Those who expect to reap the blessings
of freedom, must, like men,
undergo the fatigue of supporting it.

~ Thomas Paine

NO. 149

He that would make his own liberty secure
must guard even his enemy from oppression:
for if he violates this duty he establishes
a precedent that will reach to himself.

~ Thomas Paine

NO. 150

Arms discourage and keep the invader
and plunderer in awe, and preserve order
in the world as well as property.

~ Thomas Paine

NO. 151

Government, even in its best state,
is but a necessary evil:
in its worst state, an intolerable one.

~ Thomas Paine

NO. 152

An army of principles can penetrate where an army of soldiers cannot.

~ Thomas Paine

NO. 153

Lead, follow, or get out of the way.

~ Thomas Paine

NO. 154

It is the duty of the patriot to protect his country from his government.

~ Thomas Paine

NO. 155

These are the times that try men's souls.
The summer soldier and the sunshine patriot will,
in this crisis, shrink from the service of their country:
but he that stands it now, deserves the love
and thanks of man and women.

~ Thomas Paine

NO. 156

Tyranny, like hell, is not easily conquered;
yet we have this consolation with us,
that the harder the conflict,
the more glorious the triumph.

~ Thomas Paine

Thomas Sowell
American Economist

NO. 157

It is amazing how many people seem to think
that the government exists to turn
prejudices into laws.

~ Thomas Sowell

NO. 158

Politics is the art of making your selfish desires
seem like the national interest.

~ Thomas Sowell

Thurgood Marshall
1908-1993
United States Supreme Court Justice

NO. 159

History teaches us that grave threats to liberty often come in times of urgency, when constitutional rights seem too extravagant to endure.

~ Thurgood Marshall

Ulysses S. Grant
1822-1885
18th American President

NO. 160

Our great modern Republic. May those
who seek the blessings of its institutions
and protection of its flag remember
the obligations they impose.

~ Ulysses S. Grant

Wendell L. Wilkie
1892-1944
Presidential Candidate

NO. 161

I believe in America because we have great dreams -
and because we have the opportunity
to make those dreams come true.

~ Wendell L. Wilkie

William Ellery Channing
1780-1842
American Unitarian Preacher

NO. 162

The office of government is not to confer happiness, but to give men the opportunity to work out happiness for themselves.

~ William Ellery Channing

William J. Clinton
42nd American President

NO. 163

There is nothing wrong with America
that cannot be cured by what is right
with America.

~ William J. Clinton

William Faulkner
1897-1962
American Novelist

NO. 164

We must be free not because we claim
freedom, but because we practice it.

~ William Faulkner

Will Rogers
1879-1935
American Cowboy, Comedian & Humorist

NO. 165

It is a good thing that we do not get
as much government as we pay for.

~ Will Rogers

Winston Churchill
1874-1965
British Prime Minister

NO. 166

We contend that for a nation to try to tax itself
into prosperity is like a man standing in a bucket
and trying to lift himself up by the handle.

~ Winston Churchill

Woodrow Wilson
1856-1924
28th American President

NO. 167

Liberty has never come from the government.
Liberty has always come from the subjects of it.
The history of liberty is a history of resistance.

~ Woodrow Wilson

NO. 168

Some Americans need hyphens in their names,
because only part of them has come over;
but when the whole man has come over, heart and thought
and all, the hyphen drops of its own weight out of his name.

~ Woodrow Wilson

NO. 169

The American Revolution was a beginning,
not a consummation.

~ Woodrow Wilson

NO. 170

I prefer liberty with danger
to peace with slavery.

~ Anonymous

NO. 171

When government is big enough
to provide you everything, it is big enough
to take everything.

~ Anonymous

NO. 172

A penny saved...
is a penny taxed.

~ Anonymous

NO. 173

Congress has the unsolved problem of how
to get the people to pay taxes they can't afford
for the services they don't need.

~ Anonymous

NO. 174

You really can't beat the game...
if you earn anything it is minus taxes...
if you buy anything it's plus taxes.

~ Anonymous

NO. 175

We wonder why they call them "tax returns"
when so little of it does.

~ Anonymous

NO. 176

Ambition in America is still rewarded...
with higher taxes.

~ Anonymous

NO. 177

Freedom is never free.

~ Anonymous

Declaration of Independence
July 4, 1776

Here is the complete text of the Declaration of Independence. The original spelling and capitalization have been retained.

In CONGRESS, July 4, 1776.

A DECLARATION

By the REPRESENTATIVES of the

UNITED STATES OF AMERICA,

In GENERAL CONGRESS Assembled.

WHEN in the Course of human Events, it becomes necessary for one People to dissolve the Political Bands which have connected them with another, and to assume among the Powers of the Earth, the separate and equal Station to which the Laws of Nature and of Nature's God entitle them, a decent Respect to the Opinions of Mankind requires that they should declare the causes which impel them to the Separation.

We hold these Truths to be self-evident, that all Men are created equal, that they are endowed by their Creator with certain unalienable Rights, that among these are Life, Liberty, and the Pursuit of Happiness...

Signed by Order and in Behalf of the Congress,

JOHN HANCOCK, President.

Attest.
CHARLES THOMSON, Secretary.

Declaration of Independence

IN CONGRESS, JULY 4, 1776.

A DECLARATION

BY THE REPRESENTATIVES OF THE

UNITED STATES OF AMERICA,

IN GENERAL CONGRESS ASSEMBLED.

When in the Course of human events, it becomes necessary for one people to dissolve the political bands which have connected them with another, and to assume among the powers of the earth, the separate and equal station to which the Laws of Nature and of Nature's God entitle them, a decent respect to the opinions of mankind requires that they should declare the causes which impel them to the separation.

We hold these truths to be self-evident, that all men are created equal, that they are endowed by their Creator with certain unalienable rights, that among these are life, liberty and the pursuit of happiness. That to secure these rights, governments are instituted among men, deriving their just powers from the consent of the governed. That whenever any form of government becomes destructive to these ends, it is the right of the people to alter or to abolish it, and to institute new government, laying its foundation on such principles and organizing its powers in such form, as to them shall seem most likely to effect their safety and happiness. Prudence, indeed, will dictate that governments long established should not be changed for light and transient causes; and accordingly all experience hath shown that mankind are more disposed to suffer, while evils are sufferable, than to right themselves by abolishing the forms to which they are accustomed. But when a long train of abuses and usurpations, pursuing invariably the same object evinces a design to reduce them under absolute despotism, it is their right, it is their duty, to throw off such government, and to provide new guards for their future security. Such has been the patient sufferance of these colonies; and such is now the necessity which constrains them to alter their former systems of government. The history of the present King of Great Britain is a history of repeated injuries and usurpations, all having in direct object the establishment of an absolute tyranny over these states. To prove this, let facts be submitted to a candid world.

He has refused his assent to laws, the most wholesome and necessary for the public good.

He has forbidden his governors to pass laws of immediate and pressing importance, unless suspended in their operation till his assent should be obtained; and when so suspended, he has utterly neglected to attend to them.

He has refused to pass other laws for the accommodation of large districts of people, unless those people would relinquish the right of representation in the legislature, a right inestimable to them and formidable to tyrants only.

He has called together legislative bodies at places unusual, uncomfortable, and distant from the depository of their public records, for the sole purpose of fatiguing them into compliance with his measures.

He has dissolved representative houses repeatedly, for opposing with manly firmness his invasions on the rights of the people.

He has refused for a long time, after such dissolutions, to cause others to be elected; whereby the legislative powers, incapable of annihilation, have returned to the people at large for their exercise; the state remaining in the meantime exposed to all the dangers of invasion from without, and convulsions within.

He has endeavored to prevent the population of these states; for that purpose obstructing the laws for naturalization of foreigners; refusing to pass others to encourage their migration hither, and raising the conditions of new appropriations of lands.

He has obstructed the administration of justice, by refusing his assent to laws for establishing judiciary powers.

He has made judges dependent on his will alone, for the tenure of their offices, and the amount and payment of their salaries.

He has erected a multitude of new offices, and sent hither swarms of officers to harass our people, and eat out their substance.

He has kept among us, in times of peace, standing armies without the consent of our legislature.

He has affected to render the military independent of and superior to civil power.

He has combined with others to subject us to a jurisdiction foreign to our constitution, and unacknowledged by our laws; giving his assent to their acts of pretended legislation:

For quartering large bodies of armed troops among us:

For protecting them, by mock trial, from punishment for any murders which they should commit on the inhabitants of these states:

For cutting off our trade with all parts of the world:

For imposing taxes on us without our consent:

For depriving us in many cases, of the benefits of trial by jury:

For transporting us beyond seas to be tried for pretended offenses:

For abolishing the free system of English laws in a neighboring province, establishing therein an arbitrary government, and enlarging its boundaries so as to render it at once an example and fit instrument for introducing the same absolute rule in these colonies:

For taking away our charters, abolishing our most valuable laws, and altering fundamentally the forms of our governments:

For suspending our own legislatures, and declaring themselves invested with power to legislate for us in all cases whatsoever.

He has abdicated government here, by declaring us out of his protection and waging war against us.

He has plundered our seas, ravaged our coasts, burned our towns, and destroyed the lives of our people.

He is at this time transporting large armies of foreign mercenaries to complete the works of death, desolation and tyranny, already begun with circumstances of cruelty and perfidy scarcely paralleled in the most barbarous ages, and totally unworthy the head of a civilized nation.

He has constrained our fellow citizens taken captive on the high seas to bear arms against their country, to become the executioners of their friends and brethren, or to fall themselves by their hands.

He has excited domestic insurrections amongst us, and has endeavored to bring on the inhabitants of our frontiers, the merciless Indian savages, whose known rule of warfare, is undistinguished destruction of all ages, sexes and conditions.

In every stage of these oppressions we have petitioned for redress in the most humble terms: our repeated petitions have been answered only by repeated injury. A prince, whose character is thus marked by every act which may define a tyrant, is unfit to be the ruler of a free people.

Nor have we been wanting in attention to our British brethren. We have warned them from time to time of attempts by their legislature to extend an unwarrantable jurisdiction over us. We have reminded them of the circumstances of our emigration and settlement here. We have appealed to their native justice and magnanimity, and we have conjured them by the ties of our common kindred to disavow these usurpations, which, would inevitably interrupt our connections and correspondence. They too have been deaf to the voice of justice and of consanguinity. We must, therefore, acquiesce in the necessity, which denounces our separation, and hold them, as we hold the rest of mankind, enemies in war, in peace, friends.

We, therefore, the representatives of the United States of America, in General Congress, assembled, appealing to the Supreme Judge of the world for the rectitude of our intentions, do, in the name, and by the authority of the good people of these colonies, solemnly publish and declare, that these united colonies are, and of right ought to be free and independent states; that they are absolved from all allegiance to the British Crown, and that all political connection between them and the state of Great Britain, is and ought to be totally dissolved; and that as free and independent states, they have full power to levy war, conclude peace, contract alliances, establish commerce, and to do all other acts and things which independent states may of right do. And for the support of this declaration, with a firm reliance on the protection of Divine Providence, we mutually pledge to each other our lives, our fortunes and our sacred honor.

Signed by ORDER and in BEHALF of the CONGRESS,
JOHN HANCOCK, PRESIDENT

About The Author

R. Blake Wilson

R. Blake Wilson is a husband, father, corporate employee, small business owner, farmer and American Patriot.

Born and raised in Springfield, Illinois in the shadow of Abraham Lincoln and having achieved success and failure chasing the American Dream, Blake has grown to appreciate and admire the American story. Blake believes the time is now to stand up against tyranny in America.

DON'T TREAD ON ME ~ An American Patriot's Book of Quotes is his way of standing up for liberty and freedom in America.